I0198226

Daniel H. Morrison

**Pastime in the national Soldier's Homes**

Daniel H. Morrison

**Pastime in the national Soldier's Homes**

ISBN/EAN: 9783337135386

Printed in Europe, USA, Canada, Australia, Japan

Cover: Foto ©ninafisch / pixelio.de

More available books at **www.hansebooks.com**

PASTIME IN THE

# NATIONAL SOLDIER'S HOMES,

Of Central Branch, Dayton, Ohio, and Northwestern,
Milwaukee, Wis.

## DANIEL H. MORRISON,

Gen'l W. S. Hancock.

# RHYMING SOLDIER,

*A Citizen of the United States.*

PRICE, 25 CENTS.

PASTIME IN THE

# NATIONAL SOLDIER'S HOMES,

Of Central Branch, Dayton, Ohio, and Northwestern,
Milwaukee, Wis.

DANIEL H. MORRISON,

# RHYMING SOLDIER,

*A Citizen of the United States.*

PRICE, 25 CENTS

ERIE, PA.,
HERALD PRINTING AND PUBLISHING CO., LT'D,
1886

Copyrighted, 1886.

# REFERENCE.

Olena, Huron Co., Ohio, Aug. 8th, '80.

We, the undersigned citizens of Olena, have listened to the speech of D. H. Morrison on the Disabled Soldiers and their National Soldier's Home. We express satisfaction, and cheerfully recommend him to all, especially to the clergy, and all friends of temperance and morality.

Rev. J. P. Islip,
Mary Burns,
Eliza Williams,
T. Shipley,
L. Manahan.

# PREFACE.

The author places before the public a small part of his pastime in the Soldier's Home of Milwaukee, Wis., and Dayton, Ohio. He does not pretend every word is perfect, but he asks all to read and judge the tree by its fruit. His great wish is to advance the good cause of religion and temperance. Also a word to all comrades that have fought for the bright old flag that waves triumphant o'er our glorious Republic, United States of America,

Your obedient servant,

DANIEL H. MORRISON,

Rhyming soldier Twelfth Mich. Vol. Inf., G. A. R.

Chant 1.

## Can We Forget?

Comrades can we forget the cannon's roar
And all our battles fought from shore to shore,
While our triumphant flag so well displays
All our victories won in former days.

Chant 2.

## Dear Uncle Samuel Speaks.

Disastrous storms have raged o'er the mighty deep,
But disastrous storms caught U. S. not asleep ;
Beware of your colors, loyalty is high :
Ail colors must wave for loyalty and I.

Chant 3.

## In Memory of Our Gallant Comrades Dead.

In the grave many gallant comrades lie,
Once they marched o'er water and mountains high ;
All their brave fighting is forever done,
Their bright deeds prove effulgent as the sun.

Chant 4.

## Chanting Defined

1 Grandest of thoughts will ever rise,
  From chanting to the heavenly skies :
  God's commandments given to all,
  Will rule the world though the nations fall.

2 Chant enlightens without measure,
  Chanting guards the heavenly treasure.
  Of all the writings known condensed
  Is chanting justly recompensed.

Chant 5.

## Friendship for the Lonely.

1 My dearest friend within your sphere,
  Just now please lend a listening ear;
  All need dear friends along their way
  To guard each other night and day.

2 Should weak decisions now be no
   'Mid summer's mud and winter's snow;
   In trying times we all can name
   In winter's snow and summer's rain.

3 Sure as you read these truthful words,
   I'll watch as shepard's o'er great herds,
   And listen for the lonely voice,
   To cheer the lonely in their house.

4 Ah ! lonely friend make smooth your way,
   Choose friendship of the brightest ray,
   And share the most effulgent light,
   'Twill cheer the family circle bright.

5 All selfishness should surely yield
   To wants of home and ever shield.
   Those sailing o'er life's raging sea,
   A blessing prove triumphantly.

6 Perchance these feeble words will meet
   Pure honest eyes that ever treat,
   On loneliness, both night and day ;
   Now please discern the brightest ray.

7 Cheer up, for you can find a friend
 - Through life's great journey to the end,
   To row the boat o'er life's dark sea,
   With willing hands most cheerfully.

8 The slender vine bedecks so bright
   . The loving home a pleasant sight;
   Where friendship trails no flowers falls.
   Love trails the vine o'er flowers all.

9 Now, as I close this fleeting brief,
   None should despair in some relief ;
   The lonely fan life's glowing spark,
   Till joyful light dispels the dark.

Chant 6.

## Dakota's Prairie Bedecked With Jewels.

1 In December, eighteen and eighty-two,
   One morning very cold and frosty, too,
   Prairie grass waved and sparkled bright,
   Profusely with bright gems, a lovely sight.

2 All was silent, no interruption near
   To mar this view of delight, nought to fear ;
   Spears of grass bedecked with gems so bright,
   Oh, did fairies bedeck them in the night ?

3 Could you have seen the gems of silver light,
   As glittering gems shed forth their rays so bright,
   And were accompanied with rays of gold,
   As gems shed forth their lustre bright and cold.

4 In ectasy of joy you would have said
   Dakota's prairie a diamond bed,
   Far, far this dazzling beauty doth extend,
   As my way through those brilliant diamonds wend

5 All spears laden with dazzling beauty bend,
   Speedily the sun their beauty will end.
   Methinks those gems appear in bright array
   To cheer all lonely souls that come their way.

6 Politely all spears seem to courtesy fair,
   To the young and aged with silver hair.
   Cold, unrelenting frost such beauty give,
   One of Nature's endowments while we live.

7 Frost of many winters tinge my hair,
   As I stroll I think of the young and fair ;
   Many winters will change their youthful hue,
   Yes, winter's frost will silver their heads, too.

8 As the sun melts the shining frost so bright,
  Just so the sands of life run day and night.
  With me look across on the other shore,
  Heaven's gems appear brighter than before.

9 All of Heaven's bright gems forever last,
  In the city of gems there is no caste ;
  The poor can share with Heaven's gems so fair,
  For no respect of persons is known there.

Chant 7.

## The Rhyming Soldier's Chant on Gen. U. S. Grant.

1 Sad news to all is swiftly borne.
  Throughout this world all nations mourn,
  Throughout this world all nations read—
  *One hero less will mount his steed.*

2 Of Grant's bright deeds we'll mention few,
  Of Grant's bright deeds a brief review.
  Acme of nations fame he gained,
  *Our hero, Grant, is rightly named.*

3 Ranks of brave men at Shiloh broke.
  In thundering tones our hero spoke—
  We ne'er surrender to such men,
  *We fight for freemen's brightest gem.*

4 At Donaldson we hear no more
  Those thundering cannons as before.
  As in past days when souls were tried,
  *When foes did yield to Grant defied.*

5 Our hero, Grant, said now march on !
  Our bird with honor we must don.
  Vicksburg so great, that loving town,
  Vicksburg so great we'll tumble down.

6 Says Grant to Sherman : You must go
Through hostile towns and lay them low.
From sweet Atlanta, now be sure,
*Take hostile towns, they are impure.*

7 Gibralter Richmond Grant will strike,
And Petersburg their guns we'll spike.
Then General Lee will have to yield,
Then all his men 'll leave the field.

8 Ah, darling Richmond, Southern *Queen*,
Long have you been our loving *theme*. ·
Sweet, *loving Appomattox*, too,
*All Southern towns, we all love you.*

9 Mandate of death all must obey,
Mortality in tombs must lay.
Brave Grant's bright deeds will never die.
*Grant's deeds are lasting as the sky.*

10 All nations mourn for U. S. Grant.
Our chieftain freedom's *seed did plant*
To grow and thrive as *God may will*,
*The hero's mission, hero's fill.*

11 *All friends on earth this comrade hear*
Brave worldly storms and never fear.
Seek Jesus for your lasting guide,
*He'll lead you through both storm and tide.*

12 Wipe off the tears of hero's friends.
And pray our Lord forever sends
His blessed boon to friends so dear,
For Grant we shed the silent tear.

Chant 8.

## General Hancock.

1  We hear the tolling of the bell,
   Another hero now has fell.
   They're falling fast, the time is near,
   In vain we'll sound the roll call here.

2  Hancock, our hero once so brave,
   Is lying low within his grave.
   He's left us here on earth alone,
   Our hero's death all do bemoan.

3  He won his honored laurel bright,
   At Gettysburg, in that great fight.
   In all his other battles, too,
   He waved his sword and fought right through.

4 He faultered not, he knew no fright,
   He chose the thickest of the fight.
   He proved so faithful and so true,
   No work too great for him to do.

5 He rose in rank a shining light,
   Until he reached the greatest height.
   His record proves so very grand,
   One of the greatest in our land.

6 And now a word to friends that mourn,
   Our condolence to you is borne ;
   We soothe the loss of hero's friends,
   While we are here, but time all ends.

7 All mortals known must surely die,
   A warning great for you and I,
   And as we journey here below,
   Sure time lays all her heroes low.

8 Hancock so brave a beacon here,
   He won the prize we cherish dear.
   It's freedom's prize for black and white,
   But now he rests where is no night.

Chant 9.

## The Loyal Chant for General Butler.

1 Methinks I hear cannon loudly roar
   Near brave Jackson's battle field of yore.
   Cannons thundering at New Orleans,
   With pride we point to those battle scenes.

2 Our hero, Butler, commanded there
   His great victory he won so fair.
   All his soldiers were brave, loyal men;
   Butler taught his foes a lesson then.

3 He fought the same as Jackson of yore,
   When we left Packenham in his gore.
   Butler's victory won near the same ;
   Now enrolled on the page of fame.

4 No gaudy butterflies could misguide
   General Butler, our country's pride.
   All charming rebels Butler found there
   Of his sweet loyal dose got a share.

5 All those pretty damsels cry now hark,
   Says Brave Butler, you must toe the mark,
   Why did you the Mississippi roil ?
   No sweet rebels can our country spoil.

6 Why, la me, we'll do just as we please ;
   We've done just so for many years,
   Except in the west with brave John Brown ;
   We hung that good soul at Harper's Town.

7 La, me, sweet damsels of brilliant mirth,
   You've strewn your wickedness o'er this earth.
   No slavery shall curse a single hearth,
   Now your cursed slavery proves a dearth.

8 Up speaks those bright belles of New Orleans,
   Why, Butler's picture, how rough it seems ;
   My picture's smooth and handsome, you know,
   How can you Southern birds sing just so ?

9 Those bright, charming ladies cry dear me,
   How can we autocrats ever be ?
   Subservient to that Butler rough,
   We great autocrats want no such stuff.

10 In the mad-house you sweet birds shall go,
   Sweetest loving maids on earth below.
   But without a change you cannot climb
   To John Brown's good soul that happy clime.

11 La! me, what will the South ever do?
   Butler's picture so rough, humbly, too;
   All our slave dishes are upside down
   For hanging that precious soul, John Brown.

12 Sweet charming rebels of Southern song,
   Your sweet song of treason is too long;
   You are stiff necked, but now must bend,
   Your slavery has brought you to this end.

13 God's boon from Heaven to all so dear
   Abolishes slavery, wipes the tear;
   God's angel records o'er every door,
   No human bondage is left in store.

14 All Christian folks in this world now say,
   General Butler, hero of his day,
   Lit the gospel taper with his means,
   In the darkest region, New Orleans.

Chant 10.
## Independence.

1 Base of independence we speak of thee,
   Philadelphia base of sweet liberty:
   Where the British yoke of oppression fell,
   Thus rang to the world independence bell.

2 In Carpenter's Hall of historic age,
   Carpenter's Hall illumined by sage.
   Where founders of our Republic arose,
   Enemies of freedom they did oppose.

3 Brave men beheld the shrine of freedom bright,
   And o'er that shrine they hung freedom's bright
     light,
   Pledging their lives and all for liberty,
   Viewing freedom's bright ray of purity.

4　It was there John Dickinson led that band,
　　For God and humanity in our land.
　　There Peyton Randolph arose in great might,
　　Reviewing their grievance in thrilling light.

5　Then independence bell rang very loud,
　　King George heard it and saw the threatening cloud.
　　As times grew dark King George no more could see
　　Across the wide ocean sweet liberty.

6　In Independence Hall that daring band
　　Declared independence for our land.
　　What Jefferson began they did complete,
　　The work of that gallant band was replete.

7　Now give me liberty or give me death,
　　Indelible is Henry's motto left.
　　A wonderful act it was then and there,
　　To ring the bell as Hancock left the chair.

8　Henry's great motto forever will speak,
　　Through Heaven's bright rays it ever doth streak.
　　What our fathers have done none can undo,
　　Thus reads the world in ethereal blue.

9　Bright star of freedom Lafayette of yore,
　　With brave soldiers came from the other shore.
　　Our Eagle perched high screamed with joy,
　　Lion aghast saw the Eagle ahoy.

10　General Washington deep in thought,
　　Determined to conquer those they fought.
　　British supremacy they overthrew,
　　Giving the British Lion his just due.

11　Once more the mad Lion did loudly roar,
　　Our Eagle bade hush till all was o'er.
　　On Lake Erie where all was fierce and blue,
　　The same with great battles our country through.

12 Next was the land where cactus doth grow,
   Every battle we won with hearts aglow.
   The Mexicans suffered great defeat,
   Our fighting all Mexicans was complete.

13 Next was a pitiful cry, loud and long,
   But at last from Heaven we heard this song :
   The white, the black, the bond and the free,
   Are all the same with God this world shall see.

14 God's angel descends breaking slave chains,
   Then rising heavenward, freedom proclaims.
   Waving Lincoln's emancipation free,
   O'er this land of freedom from sea to sea.

15 Cursed slavery is past, our country will rest,
   From bondage, from ruin, from Satan's behests.
   Thousands have died that freedom might rule,
   Wiping out slavery and granting free school.

16 Great poets may write, wise judges decree,
   But none are greater than warriors free.
   Christian warriors freeing black and white,
   No mortals are greater in God's pure sight.

17 All the brightest lights of enduring fame,
   Are brilliant lights in humanity's name.
   Comrades that quelled our enemies' ire,
   Load freedom's wonderful gun, once more fire.

18 Our banner waves high in Heaven's pure air,
   World's brightest emblems with folds so fair.
   God's angel has placed within its folds,
   God's message from on high that ever holds.

19 God's message reads :  All mortals prove just,
   That all the living each other may trust.
   All living souls prove kind, honest and true,
   God's message waves with the red, white and blue.

## The Rhyming Soldiers' Chant on the Capitol of the United States.

1 The pride of our Republic so grand,
   Is Washington, the pride of our land,
   Sons of freedom behold it with pride,
   Our Washington by fire was tried.

2 Washington its lustre doth shed
   O'er living and illustrious dead.
   Its lustre extends to all known land,
   To the most remote so very grand.

3 Our Washington of freedom so bright,
   Memorial of freedom's bright light.
   With joy all hail the National dome,
   Its effulgence on all Nations has shone.

4 The Potomac's tide is passing on
   By the place of question pro. and con.
   The famous site George Washington chose,
   The famous stream by Mount Vernon flows.

5 All brilliant deeds of immortal age,
   Indelible on the world's wide stage;
   While some are climbing the hill of fame,
   Such with great honor are known by name.

6 The acme of Nation's fame so bright,
   Which eradiates our country's light;
   While the Nation sings in God we trust,
   Our triumphant flag waves true and just.

7 Our Capitol's dome so very high,
   Freedom's bright laurel for you and I;
   For ever known by all powers great,
   Land of freedom united in state.

8 From our Capitol's dome so very high,
　We view surroundings that please the eye;
　Surroundings dear to our Nation's home,
　No justice portrays all from its dome?

9 Columbia writes the Nation's prize
　On the Nation's dome where underlies,
　Independence our forefathers told,
　The world has read in letters of gold.

10 Float on bright flag of our country free,
　O'er freedom's domain from sea to sea.
　Float on bright flag in Heaven's pure breeze,
　World's purest emblem on land and seas.

11 Proudly waves our flag o'er freedom's shrine,
　Reverting thoughts to Washington's time.
　Loyal subjects reflect on the past,
　When valor hushed death's piercing blast.

Chant 12.
## Scholars and Heroes of Ancient Greece.

1 In splendor bright and dazzling hue,
　Fame points to Greece her heroes, too.
　For ever in those Grecian lines,
　Are found great deeds of ancient times.

2 Aristomenes of valor true,
　Led on those Grecian warriors few.
　Their poet, Tyrtaius, loudly sung,　·
　On the brazon house our shield ishung.

3 His songs inspired those Grecians few,
　Those Grecian soldiers thousands slew.
　At Eira then they did appear,
　The fox had led where all was drear. *

* The fox dug a hole under the walls of his cell where Aristomenes
escaped.

4 The motto of all Grecians brave,
  In Greece no bondage, Greece no slave.
  We fight for Greece, we die for Greece,
  We break slave chains, the slave release.

5 Leonidas arose and said,
  Before we yield all will be dead.
  His soldiers joined and joyfully sung
  Our rights from tyrants now be wrung.

6 Says Xerxes now a bridge of boats,
  My men go build that safely floats,
  Across the water Helespont,
  So I may reach great Athos Mount.

7 The bridge by elements was broke,
  O'er Dardanelles with sweeping stroke.
  Those builders were beheaded then,
  Three hundred of those Xerxes men.

8 The water whip and fetter, too,
  That all to Xerxes now prove true.
  A double bridge now go and build,
  With ballast great it must be filled.

9 My army, then of millions, cross
  And thunder forth a Grecian loss.
  The bridge must carry safely o'er,
  Great Xerxes army break no more.

10 Mount Athos now I'll simply take,
  Consign her to the ocean's break.
  I'll plunge her headlong in the sea,
  Why should Mount Athos hinder me

11 Give me your arm says Xerxes now
  For ever all to Xerxes bow.
  Up speaks Leonidas so brave,
  No Greek to Xerxes proves a slave.

12 Leonidas with courage true,
   Come get our arms, I say to you.
   Arrows of Xerxes hide the sun,
   Surrender Greeks, now every one.

13 Four days I'll give you now to think,
   As you stand on the dangerous brink.
   My warning take, surrender now,
   Remember all to Xerxes bow.

14 We'll fight you in the pleasant shade,
   In death our foes will now be laid.
   Six thousand Grecian soldiers the
   Slew twenty thousand Xerxes men.

15   Those Gracians fought so brave and true,
   That all were slain excepting two.
   The place is known Thermopylae,
   Those Grecians fought so valiantly.

16 Upon the sea where billows roar,
   Those Grecians fought so brave once more.
   Themestocles at Salamas fought,
   He won the prize all Grecians sought.

17 Of men and sail he had but few,
   Vain Xerxes there he did subdue.
   Once more brave Greeks vain Xerxes tries,
   Then prostrate at her feet he lies.

18 Emblazoned on the horizon,
   Alexander Great of Macedon.
   Twelve years of war that hero led,
   His last career good people dread.

19 Of all the heroes pen can name,
   There's none can vie with Grecian fame.
   Wise Solon wrote the Grecian law,
   The world in pride beheld with awe.

20  Brave Socrates her scholar bright,
    To all this world a brilliant light.
    Bright orator Demosthenes,
    All talent in this world did please.

21  Wise bards of Greece of great renown,
    Have sung their songs and handed down.
    That all may sing the fame of Greece,
    Bright thoughts confined their songs release.

22  Ah, could the mind of souls expand,
    And grasp all fame in Grecian land :
    Great pathos found in Grecian lines,
    Of ancient Greece and ancient times.

23  The wisest bards may ever write,
    Unto this world their vision bright.
    But in reflecting minds there dwell,
    Much more than poets write or tell.

24  The brightest thought may rise beyond
    The brightest orb, and may redound
    To us below for this world's good,
    So authors write as authors would.

25  But who excels those scholars bright,
    Of ancient Greece in all their might.
    Shakespeare and all may rest assured,
    None have outshone their course pursued.


Chant 13.
### The Wonderful Pen.

1   The implement of greatest wonder,
    Mid storms of lightning and thunder,
    Also peace on earth and good will to men,
    Is known to be the essential pen.

2 When the sky is clear and all is bright,
   Then with the pen it's our great delight
   To write some pleasing words to our friend,
   And in great haste the message we send.

2 How cheering those words are sure to be,
   To those dear friends we'd like to see,
   In time of trouble when help we need,
   The pen is our friend, our friend, indeed.

4 When soldiers face death and cannon roar,
   Lives depend on the pen as of yore ;
   This true message must decide our fate,
   Now speed on before it is too late.

5 All questions the pen decide with man.
   All bright scholars, too, that prove the van,
   Words certainly are inadequate
   All importance of the pen to state.

6 Without the pen no news, far or near,
   Of our Savior or friends would we hear.
   The sword, the scepter and mighty pen,
   Bear wonderful sway with all great men.

7 Search for the pen's equal far and near,
   In palaces or homes bright or drear,
   In peace or war, and you'll fail to find
   The pen's great equal for all mankind.

8 Ladies with pen have conquered, too,
   Intelligence the pen doth review,
   Talent with the pen is always bright,
   The wonderful pen, the brightest light.

Chant 14.

## The Farmer.

1 Viewing all good homes of men as we roam,
   The best home on earth is the farmer's home.
   All our sustenance comes from mother earth,
   God gives us water to save all from dearth.

2 Blessed with broad acres of fertile land,
  The farmer tills with his good faithful band;
  By the sweat of his brow he earns his bread,
  For all no hatred, much delight instead.

3 Common-sense mother earth will not forsake,
  Nought saves life but her blessings we partake,
  Our farm is our delightful home for us,
  Our farm supports and grants an overplus.

4 To feed all, great, high and low of the day,
  All should love the farmer, passing his way.
  The hunger of all he doth surely stay,
  To all living he brings earth's brightest ray.

5 The farmer's crop is pleasing to the eye,
  When the farm fails to yield we surely die.
  Do not mechanics help the farmer, too?
  Without mechanics, what would all folks do.

6 Next comes professors, in life very high.
  But without the good farmer all would die,
  Ladies, the flower of our land so bright,
  They help the husbandman, it's their delight.

7 Remember, seed time and harvest is sure;
  Without the husbandman none can endure.
  The demands of nature none can evade;
  Pride, scorn, not labor, lounging in the shade.

8 Pride goes before destruction, this nat all:
  But a haughty spirit before a fall.
  The good farmer feeds all on earth, we know,
  Thus their bright record to this world doth show.

# The Rhyming Soldier's Chant on His Homestead.

1   All alone am I in my little cot,
    In night's silent hours I awoke and thought
    Of writing something in my wakeful hours,
    Writing of this land of grain and flowers.

2   Oftimes I am sad, no friends being here,
    No bright flowers of my home circle dear;
    May God grant all my friends refreshing sleep
    Oh, such to be would be the richest treat.

3   A bright star is gleaming; it's very near,
    Methinks beckoning friends to Dakota here,
    To this fair land where all is bright and gay,
    The richest land known on the world's highway.

4   Now my promise with U. S. I must keep
    If I would reap the hay and golden wheat,
    And comply with wholesome law of our land,
    Conforming with the gift of U. S. hand.

5   Our great domain is not given away
    To those poor mortals no attention pay;
    To gratefulness all governments hold dear.
    In this land and other lands far and near.

6   I cultivate my homestead and improve,
    All of this we know my good doth behoove.
    If I would have this home I must obey,
    Some attention to U. S. I must pay.

7 On reflection a happy man am I;
    My fine home is given—I do not buy;
    God bless our government for such a gift,
    Where homesteaders may be blessed with thrift.

8    Some more of my good homestead will I write,
     And relate my anticipations bright :
     I improved my homestead ; all was right
     Before U. S. surveyor came in sight.


9    At last one day U. S. surveyor came,
     Giving me straight lines, and he took my  name ;
     My title, name and location did go
     To Washington, that Uncle Sam might know.


10   Of my squatting on a piece of his land,
     The precious gift of his generous hand,
     His surveyor, Wooley, was kind to me,
     And a gentleman he proved to be.


11   As friendly souls were bidding each farewell,
     And  Uncle Samuel's boys I wished well ;
     On straight lines they went, where  I cannot tell,
     And they left me here all alone to dwell.


12   My fine home in Dakota is my choice ;
     Some fine bird on the tree I hope will poise,
     And sing a cheering song for Uncle Sam,
     On the tree I plant for the good of  man.


13   All friends on your homesteads the same as I,
     Mind dear Uncle Samuel's call if you die.
     When U. S. calls for soldiers, falter not ;
     Our triumph flag mustn't be forgot.


14   May none pollute this fair prairie land
     With the poison that comes from Satan's hand,
     And other vices that are forbidden
     In the Holy Bible God has given.

Chant 16.

## The Lost Alpena.

ON LAKE MICHIGAN, 1880.

1 The steamer Alpena on the water so gay,
   In the harbor waiting for passengers away.
   None thought of embarking for their last resting
      place,
   While many loving friends parted with anxious face.

2 Kind friends anxious that none should meet with a
      sad fate,
   One hundred and seventy souls I wish to state,
   Not one soul was saved, O, how sad to relate,
   A deathstroke for all good friends, yes, captain and
      mate.

3 Not sure, but we think the Alpena sprung a leak,
   One hundred and seventy souls cry and shriek;
   But the deep blue waters will always be their pall,
   In Heaven we hope they rest, yes in Heaven all.

4 Now please listen, dear friends, yes fathers and
      mothers,
   Endearing friends of many sisters and brothers,
   We wish to condole all mourning for friends so dear,
   All mourning for dear friends shedding the silent tear.

5 All living mortals journeying on earth below,
   Prepare to meet your God; when he calls we must go.
   May we all sail safe o'er life's high raging billow,
   Land in Heaven, and easy will be our pillow.

6 Many dear friends have met with a watery grave;
   O, how many on the briny deep none could save,
   And all know its the same on other waters, too,
   Many crafts prove unsafe on the deep water blue.

7 Many are bereft of friends they loved so dear,
   All friends now trust in God, the future never fear.
   We never can call the dead back to life again,
   Now, all dear friends, trust in Christ, on Calvary slain.

Chant 17.

# Light.

1    Precious is the light we behold,
As dark clouds open and unfold,
Bright light eradiates from there,
Light cheers the lonely in despair.

2    Blessed boon from heaven given,
Bright light from heaven driven,
Of all lights we enjoy the most,
Is heaven's bright light with our host.

3    In our loving homes with no light
All would be sad and nothing bright;
Oh, never could we read and learn,
And compete for the golden urn.

4    Exclude bright element and glass,
In dreary dark how could we pass,
Light cheers up all as we pass on
And justly decides pro and con.

5    In Genesis the first and third,
There we find in God's blessed word,
There we find the blessing given,
Its bright light from heaven driven.

6    Better tidings we never hear
In God's word we prize so dear,
One great promise of so many,
Can any doubt? No, not any.

7    Now all dear mortals, please rehearse,
God's light of this great universe,
Our Savior, gives the warning great,
Repent before it is too late.

8    Look where you will and you'll see
All things as God says they shall be.
Falsifiers prove false no more,
God fulfills all and has of yore.

Chant 18.

## Lamented Garfield's Death.

1 The dark cloud that has hung o'er us so long
  Has dropped on sad hearts while many throng
  Around the bier of our Chief Magistrate,
  Friends pay their respect as he lies in state.

2 No mortal skill could heal the fatal wound ;
  Surgeons tested, but nothing could be found
  To save the life of our great President;
  Bright star has dropped from the firmament.

3 Viewing life's uncertain course all seems risk ;
  Unforetold death is found on life's sad disc ;
  The bright rill coursing through this world so pure,
  Quickly gone ; oh, the loss we must endure.

4 His term was very brief with us, all know ;
  No more suffering for him here below ;
  Bright intellect has gone to realms of peace,
  Garfield from all trouble God did release.

5 Inadequate are words to tell our grief ;
  For his loved ones, O, Lord, grant relief,
  His dear companion with her children bright,
  His aged mother, what a mournful sight.

6 The assassin, Charles Guiteau, did enforce,
  To death's dark regions it was Satan's course,
  Garfield's spirit rose to Heaven with joy,
  His Christian life was pure, void of alloy.

7 On his inauguration, friends he did kiss,
  With him and his loved ones all was bliss.
  Garfield committed all to God on high ;
  Friends will meet him in the sweet bye and bye.

8 Garfield to God all things did safely trust ;
  Garfield is in Heaven, for he was just ;
  Wounded, suffering, meekly did he die,
  Now gone to receive his reward on high.

Chant 19.

## Criticism.

1   A versiffer came this way
    Whose mien was mild and sad,
    With uniform so bright and gay,
    Its beauty made me glad.

2   I've traveled far since morning light,
    I'm tired now, quoth he ;
    I'd like to stop and stay all night
    And get a cup of tea.

3   Straightway we asked the stranger in
    And then a chair he took,
    And from his pocket with a grin
    He hauled a yellow book.

4   Now listen while I spread my fame,
    And you'll shortly find
    Although I have a feeble frame
    It holds a mighty mind.

5   All other Nations I defy
    To beat me on a rhyme,
    And if ye critics want to try,
    Begin it any time.

6   But when his challenge grand he read
    A tear was in our eye,
    And from our inmost heart we said
    Indeed we would not try.

7   He sang us many pretty lays
    Of knights and warriors bold,
    Of soldiers brave and galley slaves
    Of heroes young and old.

8   He stopped at last and went to bed,
    After a prayer he'd prayed,
    That God would give him daily bread,
    And other timely aid.

9  We dreamed about him all that night,
   And even in our dream,
   We saw him in the bloody fight,
   And heard his frantic screams.

10  Now when the morning light was come,
    We heard him rhyming on ;
    Some times 'twould be in quiet fun,
    Then gushing forth in song.

11  He went away with measured tread.
    And proud and scornful look,
    For after all that he had said,
    We wouldn't buy his book.

12  When stars wax dim and poets fail,
    And we are sore in need,
    His poems with delight we'll hail,
    And gladly hear him read.

                    RHYMING SCHOOL TEACHER.


Chant 20.
## Reply to the Criticism.

1  The versifier that came your way,
   You are mistaken when you say
   He hauled his book with a grin ;
   Your report is false and a sin.

2  To friends and foes I tender pay,
   My book cheers Christians on their way.
   My light for Christians I defend
   Against all trash inferiors send.

3  Christians my book do not deride,
   My mission nor much more beside.
   My book is read in Christian lands ;
   Deceive no more with heart and hands.

4   To God we sing as you show off,
    And you my Christian mission scoff.
    All Christian friends are kind to me,
    Kindness does not belong to thee.


5   My books are yellow, red and blue,
    And as you read may laugh or rue.
    Dear teacher, please correct your muse,
    And your best friends no more abuse.


6   Editors partial should not be
    Setting their type for you and me.
    God's great commands none should neglect,
    Hereafter friends treat with respect.


7   My book has proven a success,
    My most fervent prayer, may God bless
    All people known on earth below.
    My good book none can overthrow.


8   Now as all critics flutter by
    With self-esteem so very high,
    And with haughtiness look down,
    On your superiors do not frown.


9   Wipe that tear from your mournful eye,
    And right your wrongs proud buzzing fly,
    And dream no more but go to work
    From my true challenge never shirk.


10  Stars wax not dim, do poets fail,
    As they, your foolishness bewail.
    Sweet darling critic, as you stroll,
    May God turn your deceitful soul.

11  All Editors on earth below,
Sow this broadcast, that all may know
This is the time for all to try
To rhyme with me ; all I defy.

12  Dear friends, may all of this suffice,
As critics open their blind eyes,
And learn this to their heart's content,
Their trash in vain to me is sent.

RHYMING SOLDIER.

## P. S.

My dear critic I'd like to see,
Singing this to her in high glee,
All in this world please guess her name,
On land and o'er the raging main.


Chant 21.
## Beautiful Woodland Cemetery,

AT DAYTON, OHIO.

1  Can I describe this great city of the dead,
In all its loving beauty where'er I tread,
My mind enwraped in grandeur I behold,
As I read the epitaphs of young and old.

2  As I stroll I find the vale doth intervene,
Beautiful sylvan hills and the lovely scene,
Magnanimous were the founders of this place,
And many hearts in the work doth interlace.

3  From its observatory great is the view,
Dayton and her surroundings appear anew,
Woodland Cemetery we admire so grand,
With joy we shout, it's the beauty of our land.

Chant 22.

## Education.

1 Youths of all lands, attention now,
  To win the prize I'll tell you how,
  Seek education in good time,
  It's free to all in every clime.


2 It bends the twig, inclines the tree,
  That all on earth may plainly see,
  To find the way that leads to fame,
  On land and o'er the raging main.


3 'Tis education and good name,
  In storm or shine always the same.
  When storm prevails on life's rough sea,
  Your education's safe with thee.


4 When money fails and friends discard,
  The way of scholars is not hard,
  With education all is well,
  On life's bright shore where mortals dwell.


5 But with great learning and vile name,
  You'll fail to reach the highest fame.
  Your learning bright and good report,
  Will always prove your best support.


6 No ignorance binds the scholar bright,
  To falsifiers day or night,
  'Tis education rules the world,
  On the height of fame has unfurled


7 The standard known to all so true,
  The guide for all, myself and you.
  Its known the world's resplendent hue,
  When we the Christian's course pursue.

Chant 23.

## The Rhyming Soldier's Chant on the Fire Department.

1 Fireman can we sleep to-night,
Will the bell warn all out right,
Will the bell sound forth its call,
Hasten on ye firemen all.

2 When the bell warns all around,
In alarm we must be found,
Where true firemen falter not,
Is where the fire rages hot.

3 Fireman's crafty horses see,
Listening so attentively,
In alarm their horses bound,
Under their harness they're found.

4 Agile driver quick as thought.
In his seat brave driver sought.
Now alarm is sounding loud,
See the flame and smoky cloud.

5 With lightning speed on they dash,
All seems like a lightning flash,
Others join the fleety train,
Speeding on for the flame.

6 Many join the anxious throng,
Can the journey be so long.
Sounding bell all hastening by,
On the wings of speed they fly.

7 Now we hear those mortals cry,
With flame and smoke we shall die.
The Lord save all, many pray,
Will they live another day.

8 Now the ladder rises high,
  And saving all is their cry.
  All those precious souls they save,
  Honor to those firemen brave.

9 All are saved from the flame, ·
  All those precious souls they name.
  Water streaming on the fire,
  Do brave firemen ever tire.

10 Firemen with your axes there,
   Yes, pull down the building fair,
   We must save our famous town,
   With our hooks we pull it down.

11 O'er the lake Chicago's fire,
   Boston with her lofty spire.
   All lands known and raging main,
   Fire's result can mortals name.

12 Determined fire is our friend,
   Faithful servant God did send,
   Faithful servant in its place,
   Hardest master to efface.

13 Consuming flames cease their roar,
   Great destruction is all o'er,
   For a little season now
   Of the future tell us how

14 Fireman save our churches high.
   Their lofty spires please the eye,
   Point to Heaven you and I,
   Glorious sweet bye and bye.

15 Of the future now we speak,
   From the cellar to the peak.
   For your safety now look out,
   Destructive fire some may shout.

16 All brave firemen run a risk,
   Written on the fireman's list.
   Enrolled on the page of fame.
   There you find the fireman's name.

Chant 24.

## The Rhyming Soldier's Chant on Christ Church, Philadelphia.

1 How glad are we to meet in Christ Church here,
Our minds blessed with God's word we hear,
In ecstasy of joy all join and sing,
Hail Columbia Hopkinson did bring.

2 Could those old sacred walls but only speak,
And tell of those that met here once a week ;
It was Christ, sovereign balm for wounded souls,
They sought on life's rough sea that ever rolls.

3 George Washington so joyfully did come,
And dear Martha from their Mount Vernon home,
To worship with God's happy children here.
In those great meetings methinks Christ was near.

4 Illustrious statesmen were heard to say,
Kind Rector Duchie in our Congress pray,
Father of our country with friends did kneel,
Rector Duchie prayed God our wounds would heal.

5 Most innate thoughts of Christain souls arise,
For those illustrious friends beyond the skies.
Dickinson and Randolph, patriots true,
Our great Franklin and Patrick Henry too.

6 Our great patriots bade England adieu,
Blood of brave freemen gave the lasting hue,
While we enjoy sweet liberty they won,
For this fairest land 'neath the shining sun.

7 Precious boon of freedom God held in store.
For before the terrible storm was o'er,
Fiercest lightning from the heavens did melt
King George's crown hard by where it was sent.

8  Patriots in our country's youthful days,
   Chanted psalms of David, those cheerful lays.
   God decrees great changes and will always,
   For another hand this great organ plays.

9  Many Rectors have led the pious way,
   Kind Rector Foggo preaches here to-day
   From prayer book and Bible, gift of Queen Ann,
   The greatest gift known for woman and man.

10 Can we forget all dear friends meeting here,
   Dear Martha and George Washington so dear,
   As Mary of old chose the better part,
   So did our illustrious friends with pure heart.

11 On this voyage of life, Oh ! don't you see,
   Illustrious friends beckoning to you and me,
   As our Saviour waves Heaven's cheerful light,
   O'er life's sad billows, Oh ! the precious sight.

12 Within those sacred walls of ages gone,
   Would an abler pen write liberty's dawn.
   Yes, abler depict our country's first morn,
   And abler write Christ in a manger born.

Chant 25.

## Thought.

1  Jehovah has decreed it so,
   All thought that's known on earth below,
   Is free to all on life's highway—
   The darkest night, and brightest day.

2  Distinguished lights blessed with great wealth,
   Knows none can gain dear thought by stealth,
   No earthly prize secures bright thought,
   Without consent it's never bought.

3 The.poor, the rich, the proud, the gay,
  All share dear thought the brightest ray.
  Great bliss of thought none can deprive
  Most humble soul ou earth alive.

4 And when too late for souls to creep
  O'er graves of those where loved ones sleep,
  To gain bright thought that's risen high,
  Bright thought that soars above the sky.

5 The seal when placed on thoughts so true,
  Ah, should it break, so friends will rue;
  No, God forbid, it is my theme
  To keep my trust across life's stream.

6 Life's intellect with vision bright,
  Pure thought that gives a cheerful light.
  Should we divulge all thought that's known,
  Why then the seed of strife is sown.

7 Oh blessed thought so free for all,
  Though nations rise and nations fall,
  All thoughts remain a secret true,
  And yet may shine in lasting hue.

8 Ah stand aloof from world's great jar,
  Enjoy dear thought that's pure and fair,
  And when it is but just and right,
  Bind thought so it will take no flight.

9 When speech does fail and death is sure,
  Bright thought will rise to Heaven so pure,
  'Where thought may rise as Christians will,
  True is God's mandate, thought keep still.

10 In all immensity of space,
  No mortal yet has found the place
  Where thought will stop and rise no more,
  Pure thought ne'er fails to reach the shore.

11 And as we stroll on earth below,
  All thoughts may come, all thoughts may go,
  But none the wiser thought is still,
  When souls on earth pure missions fill.

Chant 26.
## Elisha and Elijah of Old.

1 Elijah great, a prophet true,
Was fed by angels ravens too,
A widow too with him did share,
Her scanty meal, her humble fare.

2 While 'neath a juniper tree he lay,
Elijah there was heard to say:
Here 'neath this tree now let me die,
My father's slain as good as I.

3 An angel touched and said arise,
This cake I place before your eyes,
You'll find some water near your head,
Now eat and drink as I've said.

4 Your journey is too great, I know,
Now eat and drink, you'll find it so,
God knows all your father's slain.
Then by the cave the Lord he came.

5 A fire too, was seen there then,
A voice was heard, 'twas not from men,
What doest thou here, Elijah true,
I know it all, I care for you.

7 Elijah great was sheltered there.
Yes, in that cave so rough and bare.
Then as the Lord was passing by,
Earthquake and wind rent mountains high.

7 Elijah proved the living God,
To Baal Elijah never bowed,
With Ahab and his wicked wife,
Elijah ended all their strife.

8 Then Yezebel the dogs did eat,
And Ahab slain no more could cheat,
Elisha then with him did go,
Translation then the Lord did show.

9 Chariot of fire and horses too,
   Of all Elisha had a view,
   Translated then to Heaven above,
   That prophet great the Lord did love.

10 Elisha left alone did see,
   Elijah then from earth was free,
   Elisha's firm and great desire,
   Was granted from the chariot of fire.

Chant 27.

## Adam and Eve in the Garden of Eden.

1 Jehoviah planted eastward there,
   The Garden Eden rich and fair.
   The river Pison there did flow,
   So fruits in Eden there could grow.

2 A man to dress and keep it, too,
   Of habits bright and morals true.
   In Eden there God placed to keep,
   To plant, and sow and then to reap.

3 God said to Adam thus alone,
   Now from your side I take a bone.
   And for your good make your help meet,
   For Adam's good thus God did treat.

4 Adam slept sound and then awoke,
   Of flesh and bone then Adam spoke.
   A man shall cleave unto his wife,
   All of his days, his natural life.

5 Adam and Eve—first mortal race—
   In Eden lived, that lovely place.
   How happy their lives would have been,
   Had they obeyed God there and then.

6 Now to avoid all sin and shame,
   From God the great commandment came.
   Fruits of all trees now you may eat,
   Excepting one I thus entreat.

7 Eat not of that or you'll die,
    Obey your God he rules on high.
    The subtle serpent came that way,
    Eat fruit forbidden live I say.

S The serpent Eve did then deceive,
    Then Adam, too, did Eve believe.
    Fruit God forbid they then did eat,
    Those two then saw and knew deceit.

9 The Lord made coats to cover shame,
    God cared for them they were to blame.
    In Eden there when it was cool.
    They heard the Lord, they heard his rule.

10 Just as God said, it proved the same,
    A trusty sword of burning flame.
    A cherubim did then display,
    This sword to keep them far away.

11 A ransom then for all did come,
    Christ Jesus from his Nazerath home,
    That we may live our Savior died,
    In Jesus live with him abide.

Chant 28.

## Christ's Ascension.

1 Of Christ's ascension join and sing,
    Such cheerful tidings angels bring.
    Christ rose from earth to Heaven high,
    To intercede for you and I.

2 Two Marys at Christ's tomb were seen,
    Soon as the morning light did gleam.
    They wished to see where Christ was lain,
    Our Savior, Christ, who had been slain.

3 The Lord had sent His angel fair
    To roll the stone found lying there,
    From Christ's lone tomb, so they could see
    Our Savior, Christ, from earth was free.

4 God's angel spake 'mid lightning flame,
  To those dear women when they came;
  Dear Christ has risen, he's not here,
  To Heaven ascended, do not fear.

5 That angel's face, white as the snow,
  Spoke thus to those fair ones below.
  For they sought Jesus crucified,
  Same Jesus Christ men had defied.

6 God's angel bade those women go
  To Galilee and let them know
  Christ soon would be in Galilee,
  And there His brethren He would see.

7 Then as they ran with joy and fear,
  They met dear Christ, for He was near
  And as they met Christ said all hail,
  Great joy with them did then prevail.

8 May Christ our captain ever be,
  He leads poor souls, he leads them free,
  To Paradise, and crowns them then
  With Zion's brilliant diadem.

Chant 29.

## U. S. Challenge.

1 Now, dear soldier, at your great work you must go,
  And your Nation's great ability you must show,
  Your Nation's great challenge you must contrive,
  And to excel, defy all Nation's alive.

2 Now, all know my truthful challenge is complete,
  Now, dear mortals, never despair as you compete,
  O, beware; in case you fail, all will deride,
  And the referee her face with shame will hide.

3 I challenge all wise heads in this great world,
  Yes, all wisest heads, straight or nicely curled,
  To excel the challenge of my Nation's pen,
  For when my Nation writes, O, victory then!

4 The great challenge of U. S. we did receive,
  March twelfth, eighty we read and do believe,
  Said great challenge assumes all here below,
  And now, to excel another world we go.

5 Now we go and find beautiful, charming, wise,
  And as she reads, in great anger she replies :
  Dear mortals, when you lack wisdom keep from here,
  And trouble me not, your wisest, pretty dear.

6 Dear Nation shame for all to make such ado,
  Inferiors expose their ignorance, too,
  All keep from here, and bother me no more,
  That great Nation U. S., I love and do adore.

7 Uncle Sam, mentally, is too great for you,
  And his wonderful army of millions, too.
  With Uncle Sam you never can compete,
  And his brave eagle you never can defeat.

Chant 30.

## Jacob's Ladder.

1 Jacob dreamed of a ladder high,
  It reached from the ground to the sky.
  It reached from the ground, far above
  To Heaven, where all is joy and love.

2 The ladder angels descend and call,
  And ascend, inviting people all,
  Of that loving scene I tell you, now,
  As dear angels soothe the Christian's brow.

3 The Lord spake from the ladder above,
  God spake from on high, his words were love :
  The land where thou liest is yours now,
  For dear Jacob and his kin I vow.

4 Jacob's kin shall live both east and west,
  Also north and south and all be blest;
  The Lord with Jacob will surely be,
  And from all danger will now keep thee.

5   I'll bring thee again into this land,
    That all things may prosper in thy hand;
    This place is the Lord's, I knew it not,
    So near Heaven, can it be forgot.

6   Jacob said, this is God's house, I see,
    And the gate of Heaven it must be ;
    Jacob rose early in the morning,
    Before the bright sun was adorning.

7   Oil he poured on his stone pillar,
    With Bethel all might be familiar ;
    Jacob says if my God will keep me
    Then my good Lord He shall surely be.

8   In father's house may I rest in peace
    And from all trouble may God release,
    And my stone pillar God's house shall be,
    And one-tenth of mine I'll now give thee.

9   Jacob journeyed and found a well,
    As they talk of Laban's flock and tell,
    And all were conversing Rachel came,
    Now Jacob tells Rachel kin and name

10   Laban pleased to see Jacob, too ;
    Now, dear Jacob, how shall I pay you ?
    Seven years for lovely Rachel dear,
    Seven years I'll labor for her here.

11   Many times things are strange for awhile,
    As time rolls on and some would beguile,
    For Lehi, too, Jacob labors long ;
    To faithful Jacob much does belong.

12   Laban, says, Jacob, now I pray thee
    To journey not, but tarry with me ;
    More enjoyment and profit for you
    To share with cattle, sheep and goats, too.

13    Many colors of cattle display,
      Good cattle, sheep and goats I'll pay;
      Jacob makes a good selection, too,
      For Jacob the feeble would not do.

14    Of Jacob and his good kin of old,
      Of them much more in truth could be told,
      But I close by warning all to heed
      The moral of this lesson we read.

MORAL—Jacob's moral, Christian friends, is this:
          Prove God's children, and all will be bliss.
          God gave Jacob all where he did lie;
          Angels viewed all with a loving eye.

Chant 31.

## Joseph of Old.

1    Joseph was Jacob's bright son of old,
     He was feeding the flock, I am told,
     When his age was only seventeen,
     A good young man by all 'll be seen.

2    Of his brethren he reported bad;
     Of such we find his brethren felt sad.
     Joseph was loved more than the rest;
     Now Joseph by his father was blest.

3    Good Jacob's love for Joseph was great,
     His jealous brethren Joseph did hate.
     Of many colors his coat was made;
     His dream before his brethren was laid.

4    For in the field we were binding sheaves,
     My sheaf arose and stood up with ease.
     Yours stood around and bowed to mine.
     Shaltthou reign o'er us and all be thine?

5   His brethren hated him more indeed,
Says Joseph another dream now heed,
Sun, moon and stars surely bowed to me,
O, such a sight could we only see.

6   Says father, must we bow to the earth ?
None thought of the great forthcoming dearth.
Joseph now sought his brethren afar,
His brethren thought to slay Joseph there.

7   When dead what will become of his dreams,
To slay Joseph, too wicked it seems,
We better cast him into some pit.
All this they done in a jealous fit

8   His coat of many colors they took,
Dipped it in blood, a chilling look,
As they ate they lifted up their eyes,
They sold Joseph, money was their prize.

9   Twenty pieces of silver in all,
For their good brother, and their downfall.
Reuben returned, the child is not,
His bloody coat is all we've got.

10   His father said it's my son's coat,
The blood is my son's, not of a goat.
A beast has killed my son so pure,
O, can I such great trouble endure.

11   Many times we think of persons vile,
And the innocent they would beguile,
Joseph was imprisoned, we know,
No mercy on him did foes bestow.

12   The Lord was kind to Joseph again,
With foes he had proven so humane;
Such is the case with all proving good,
Joseph favored his foes all he could.

13    King Pharaoh was much wroth just now,
       With officers and Joseph, I vow.
       Baker and butler were in the ward
       With Joseph the man of our good Lord.

14    Chief baker and butler had dreams,
       So Joseph did interpret, it seems.
       O, why look ye so sadly to day,
       Why great dreams belong to God, I say.

15    Why, ye men, your dreams are plain to me,
       The three branches are the three days you see.
       Think of me when it is well with thee,
       Chief butler, be kind, as you should be.

16    I was stolen from the Hebrew land,
       Innocent am I in Pharaoh's hand.
       Now chief baker was in his dream, too ;
       Says Joseph, I interpret for you.

17    Why your three baskets are the three days,
       Your dream is plain but it has no rays.
       Three days more for you with no distress,
       Then hang and the birds will eat your flesh.

18    The third day Pharaoh made a feast,
       In vain, kind Joseph had sought release,
       Chief butler is restored again,
       Chief baker is hanged with much shame.

19    Chief butler was unkind, ungrateful, too,
       For his friend Joseph naught did he do.
       All kindness of Joseph he forgot,
       For kindness, no favors Joseph got.

20    King Pharaoh dreamed and then awoke,
       By the river naught my silence broke.
       Seven kine out of the river came,
       Of the seven I knew not their name.

21    Seven more and ill-favored, too,
      The lean ate the fat, now it is true,
      The same with corn; it was a great dream,
      Wise men now tell me what my dream does mean.

22    I remember my great faults this day,
      Chief butler to Pharaoh then did say,
      Then of his friend, wise Joseph, he told.
      Joseph interprets in truth and bold.

23    Send for that Joseph, I pray thee, now,
      Now, dear Joseph, do tell me how
      My great dream will prove, and soothe my brow,
      My true answer is in peace, I vow.

24    I interpret your dream of seven,
      King Pharaoh it is from Heaven.
      Now God shows Pharaoh what to do,
      King Pharaoh this is truth for you.

25    Just seven years of plenty in all,
      Next seven years of famine befall
      On all Egypt and other lands, too,
      King Pharaoh, this is truth for you.

26    O, King, now prepare for time of need,
      God's great advice all should surely heed.
      Says Pharaoh, Joseph proves discreet,
      Wise Joseph with great honor I treat.

27    Pharaoh to Joseph gave his ring,
      And to Joseph fine linen did bring,
      He put a gold chain about his neck,
      In splendor, Pharaoh did bedeck.

28    In the chariot Joseph rides, too,
      Changed is Joseph as we review.
      As great Joseph rides all bow the knee,
      In great justice God rules all we see

29    Pharaoh now gives Joseph a wife,
      With wisdom Joseph rules to save life,
      Providing for all with garners full,
      Not only grain, but much flax and wool.

30    Says father, to Egypt you must go,
      To buy corn, or we all die, you know.
      Their father's great mandate they did heed,
      Ten went to buy corn in time of need.

31    But young Benjamin I must recall,
      Peradventure some mischief may fall;
      So they left Canaan, the land of dearth,
      In Egypt they bowed to earth.

32    Good Joseph knew his brethren afar;
      Strangely now, speaks roughly to them there.
      Whence come ye, from Canaan to buy food
      That none may starve in our neighborhood?

33    Their bartered brother God did them show,
      But brother Joseph they did not know.
      God's justice with them did surely speed,
      Joseph with justice ruled indeed.

34    Joseph remembered his great dreams;
      Now to deceive, you are spies, it seems.
      We've come to buy food and are no spies,
      We are brethren and wish to save lives.

35    We are brethren, one is at home,
      One is not; but for corn we come.
      O, one is not! I judge you all spies,
      Now for truth and your brother, likewise.

36    Now send one and fetch your brother here,
      All but one in ward, three days in fear,
      If ye be true men, one stay with me,
      Others carry corn, friends, you may see.

37 Bring him to me and ye shall not die,
   In anguish they thought of God on high.
   Now guilty they were and felt ashame,
   Selling kind Joseph they were to blame.

38 I spake do not sin against the child,
   Think of all, and our brother so mild.
   Joseph their language did understand,
   Joseph turned and wept in his hand.

39 Joseph then bound Simeon strong,
   Proceed with your corn, your journey long,
   And food you must have that you may eat,
   Demands of your nature never cheat.

40 Lo! behold as I open my sack,
   Why, just see my money is sent back.
   In fear: What has God done to us?
   With news to their father they did rush.

41 As they related all their great news,
   Bereft of my children, such undoes.
   O, father, we bring them back to thee.
   Mischief may befall, child stay with me.

42 O my sorrow, his brother is dead,
   None are hungry now, corn to be fed.
   Should he not return and all behave
   With sorrow I'll go to my grave.

43 The famine waxed sore in the land,
   Our youngest is still with our good band
   So buy us more corn that we have food,
   The man protested we must prove good.

44 Now send Benjamin, if food you want,
   Ye deal ill, can you my projects daunt.
   Man asked, is your father alive?
   Now do send the lad when we arise.

45    Our little ones, we will save their lives,
Why surely then, not one of us dies,
I'll insure him back in thy hand.
Jacob now complies with their demand.

46    Double the money, such will be right,
Peradventure there was an oversight.
God give you mercy before that man,
O, bring Benjamin back if you can.

47    The men took all before Joseph now,
Bring these men all, is dearth where they plow.
The men in Joseph's house were afraid,
Their case before the steward was laid.

48    With them suspicion caused much fear,
Are we to be bondsmen? all was drear.
Tell who put that money in our sacks,
We fulfill on our part nothing lacks.

49    Steward said, peace be with you, fear not,
I had your money, no risk, no lot.
Of your father's welfare do tell me,
Now as I yearn, Benjamin I see.

50    Then Joseph in his chamber did weep,
Such as we pen this treasure we keep.
Joseph says, I wash, set on the bread,
No trouble with any, joy instead.

51    Egyptians and Hebrews now did eat,
Everyone had a separate seat.
All of Joseph's brethren ate of such,
But Benjamin had five times as much.

52    Now all ate, drank and were merry, too,
All brethren were merry as we view.
How happy those brethren must have been,
As all were safe from great famine then.

53 Says Joseph, now fill their sacks with corn,
Return their money, they start when morn,
My silver cup for the youngest, too,
Send corn and money, this you must do.

54 At daylight the men were sent away,
Now steward, follow after, I say,
And say you have done evil for good.
Steward, we would not steal if we could.

55 O, we are honest and would not steal
Your silver or gold, how sad we feel.
Search now, and who has it let him die.
Steward searched, none did him pass by.

56 Now such a strange search none could define,
Says dear Joseph, am I not divine.
Then Judah labored hard to clear
He and his brethren.   They were in fear.

57 Give us the child, our father is old,
That we fulfill our promise as told.
One good brother in pieces was torn,
Father and his children are forlorn.

58 Then Joseph by his brethren was known.
I am Joseph, from my kin I was torn,
In Egypt you sold Joseph, you know,
God sent me here, now you know it's so.

59 Haste now bring father and all to me.
All go to Goshen there all may be
I'll nourish all thou hast and thee,
Go tell father in truth as you see.

60 Joseph met his father and did weep.
Now says father: God did Joseph keep
To save us from the famine great ;
Now let me die.   Joseph none did hate.

61　Brother Benjamin I give this day
　　Much silver to help him on his way,
　　Silver three hundred pieces in all,
　　Raiment, five changes for him I call.

62　Benjamin merits this much, you know ;
　　Our love is great and was long ago.
　　Much have I given to all of you,
　　And the good Lord will visit you, too.

63　Says Joseph :　My brethren I forgive,
　　God will visit you, sure as you live ;
　　And good Canaan, you will inherit,
　　The Lord will give you all you merit.

64　Now bury me where father is laid.
　　Father, I'll do as thou hast said.
　　Now bury me by my father's side.
　　In seventeen years Jacob died.

65　When the Lord calls Joseph must go thence,
　　And ye shall carry my bones from hence.
　　Joseph's age hundred and ten years,
　　Joseph died happy and with no fears,

66　Joseph embalmed, reads holy writ,
　　And put in a coffin in Egypt.
　　All I have wrote of Jesus is true ;
　　Remember God's care, his law pursue.

67　Bright Joseph's history I close soon,
　　With Joseph all was God's bright boon.
　　The Lord was with Joseph and his kin,
　　And all were forgiven of their sin.

JOSEPH'S ENERGY IN EGYPT ILLUSTRATED.

68　The bright crystal stream that's never still,
　　And leaps in splendor from yonder hill,
　　And turns the wheel in yonder mill,
　　And great demands cheerfully fulfill,

MORAL—Joseph proved righteous and discreet,
　　　　Now all shun treachery and deceit.
　　　　All shun vice, obey God's just commands,
　　　　Surely this the good of all demands.

Chant 32.

## Sustaining the Holy Bible.

AN ANSWER TO SKEPTICS.

1 The Bible is my criterion, all know,
Fancying delusions just for a great show;
Advocating delusions for false pretense,
Assuredly ends at the sinner's expense.


2 The great fool in his heart says there is no God,
He curses all on earth, the earth he has trod.
He defies God in all his supreme power.
·He blessed, but cares naught for Heaven's shower.


3 God suffers him in great defiance to live,
He defying all great blessings God may give.
Allunbelievers will receive their just due,
An when it is too late they'll surely rue.


4 Now, all heed God's teachings, his good laws obey,
From God's great and righteous precepts never stray.
The Holy Bible all people know is true,
It heals our great wounds, includes myself and you.


5 Heaven's great treasure left with us here below,
To bless us on life s great journey as we go.
All Christians love the Bible, it is their guide
In this world and the world of spirits beside.


6 Martyrs have surrendered their lives so pure,
That the Bible for all ages might endure.
No more does the Bible demand than is right;
Why should it be removed from our sight?


7 Was any person ever known to be worse
By heeding God's law and the Bible rehearse ?
No, the worst are found who disobey God's law,
Then preceding death the Bible has no flaw.

Chant 33.
## Christ's Temperance Staff.

1 The temperance cause, with Scripture I'll found,
  Job thirty-six and first I now propound.
  Now, follow me and you'll find peace for all.
  Hebrews thirteenth and first, Christ in love doth call.

2 The first, suffer me to speak in God's behalf,
  Second, brotherly love continue our staff,
  Next, taste not when the wine is colored red,
  Thus our Heavenly Father has surely said.

3 Now the greatest of all, neither taste nor touch
  Any alcoholic drink, just think of such,
  Which your character with much disgrace will blot,
  Be sure to shun saloons and the drunken sot.

4 Now, take heed and enjoy Christ's temperance staff.
  Now all this I say in our Savior's behalf.
  Sign the temperance pledge and God will bless you.
  Live temperate; brotherly love continue.

Chant 34.
## Point of a Pin.

1 I'm told the point of a pin is much to small,
  To compose anything good or useful at all ;
  But when we consider the work it has done,
  For size and price it excels all 'neath the sun.

2 Tailors on pattern and dress their minds so fervent,
  As they employ the pin, have no better servant ;
  And the little pin helps bind all our wounds that
      ache,
  Oh, what a great blessing for humanity's sake.

3 Now, with the little pin we must be careful, too,
  In destruction our happiness it will undo.
  Many have swallowed a pin, the point did pierce,
  Then the struggle for life was very long and fierce.

4 Just a scratch of the point of the little pin,
  Has locked both jaws and terrible death within.
  Now friends, as you learn of this point I write,
  Oh, consider the great importance brought to light.

Chant 35.

## Humility.

1 Many millions of good people on this earth dwell,
But only one in millions write the poet well,
While many souls aspire for poet's honored name,
How few those poets are that reach the height of fame.


Chant 36.

## Result of War.

1 As we view transplendent military fame of yore,
And great result of war that lights all from shore to
shore.
No brighter jewel of military fame is known,
Than result of war freedom on white and black hath
sown.

2 Ah! the great rebellion of eighteen and sixty-two,
Was what tried courageous soldiers and finance, too.
As loyal soldiers fought their souls with courage fired,
God's precious boon we won of slavery we were tired

3 Illustrious heroes have removed many wrongs
From the path of freedom where all happiness belongs.
Military lights will always be distinguished,
Columbia's lights never be extinguished.

4 We know the brightest page of fame points to heroes
great,
Many wise generals ruled both army and state;
And many great heroes on the briny ocean deep,
The record of those heroes this world will ever keep.

5 Columbus sailed and sought as raging waves did toss
This wonderful discovery to us all gain loss.
His sword of our Republic is wielded with success,
Righteous God in Thee we trust; our Nation always
bless.

6 Excelsior climbs the mount mid ethereal blue,
Examining the base of all Nations as he may view.
Many Nations rise and fall and many live in fear,
The unyielding Gibralter, U. S. the Lord holds dear

Chant 37.

## Soldiers' Monument.

1 Kind friends in every state in our great Nation,
  Please listen now what 'ere may be your station:
  Our soldier's monument in majesty doth stand,
  Known the brightest memorial of our land.


2 In the service our great heroes fought and won,
  Sweet liberty, the greatest boon 'neath the sun,
  Many friends to soldiers always proving kind,
  And to soldiers no better Nation can you find.


3 The sculpter has proved proficient in his art,
  And funeral scenes of soldiers effect the heart.
  We know bright stars from the firmanent doth fall,
  The same with gallant soldiers answering their call.


4 Our monument appears resplendent over all,
  And we prize it the great memorial of the pall,
  While each brave soldier with honor fills his station,
  Loyal soldiers gained the freedom of our Nation.


5 Comrades from land and sea guard respectively
  Dear comrades signal as danger proves to be.
  Comrades hear their bugles, that bugle, comrades, hear,
  Commander shouts to arms, danger may be near.


6 Comrades hasten now, come on in double quick,
  See the foe in rank and file, their ranks so thick;
  Plant all your batteries, now give them shot and shell,
  All comrades charge, foes shall fall as others fell.

Chant 38.

# Devotion.

### THE RHMYING SOLDIER'S PRAYER.

1 There is serenity that clings around,
  Much sacredness of purpose doth abound
  Around God's alter our devotion dear,
  Much sacredness of purpose clusters near.


2 Purity is the Christian's course of life
  That rise in grandeur of thought, with no strife
  Fragrance of thought that floats upon the air,
  And falls as dew of Heaven on the fair.


3 Lord in Heaven, shower thy grace from on high
  On all, as time is passing swiftly by,
  Guide us safely in the Christian's path of light,
  Guide us to thy mansion where all is bright.


4 All sinners repent, heed our Savior's call,
  Heaven's pearly gate is open to all,
  To all seeking Christ and his laws obey.
  Heaven's cheering light guide such on their way.


5 All Christian friends on earth their trophies bring,
  Angels 'mid gleaming stars, transcendant fling,
  Canopy of Heaven lit with God's love,
  As dear angels are viewing from above.


6 All voices rise in admiration high,
  Bright angels view all with a loving eye.
  As humming birds sip nectar on the wing,
  Devotion to all good souls joy doth bring.


7 Lamp from the dome of Heaven, cheerful light,
  Guide dear friends on their way with record bright.
  Grace from on high descend on mortals all.
  Oh, may the sinner heed the Savior's call.

8 In Our Father's mansion there is no night,
　Heaven's effulgence, a glorious sight,
　Our prayers on life's sunset will joyful bloom.
　The efficient artist lines Christian's doom.

9 Chant and tell my prayer to all Nations known,
　That good seed on all good soil may be sown,
　And in God's cause produce an hundred fold,
　Friends may we meet in Heaven young and old.

Chant 39.

## Twilight on the Vast Prairie.

1　Behold the rich border of golden lace,
　　Lit with bright features of Thalia's face.
　　The western horizon is lit with fire
　　As the faithful sun recedes to retire.

2　Now fair twilight calls on the human race,
　　This great earth and immensity of space;
　　Bright Thalia lifts the curtain now
　　With her fair hand from the horizon's brow.

3　Can all worth of such harbingers be told?
　　Sages answer with true pen of old.
　　Bright twilight's mission, essential and fair,
　　Sublimely excells brilliants grand and rare.

4　Dear angels for enjoyment seem to call,
　　And fair twilight responds inviting all,
　　As she fondly clasps ethereal blue,
　　In silver light, for earth and heaven, too.

5　Dear twilight wends her way to every hearth,
　　Every hearth of sustaining mother earth.
　　Now tardily she recedes from her task.
　　Where has twilight gone? nymphs from mountain
　　　　ask.

6   Responds a fairy's voice from yonder vale:
    Rosy twilight glides o'er hill, mount and dale,
    And falls asleep in soft arms of caress,
    And when she wakes she dons her evening dress.

7   In rich hue her border of golden lace
    She spreads all o'er immensity of space,
    And as the weary sun is seeking rest,
    Mild twilight appears on the mountain's crest.

8   Now twilight in her dress of pearly hue,
    Repeats her embrace in folds of sky blue.
    As she tardily recedes from her task,
    Is dear twilight gone ? charming sirens ask.

9   The three muses of poetry now speak,
    Twilight obeys when angels bid retreat.
    She has lit the traveler on his way,
    To that yon distant lee where he may lay.

10  And Niobe, too, with loving voice responds,
    Twilight's great mission in glory redounds.
    Her bright reflection from some silver mound,
    Lights mothers where her loved ones are found.

11  Lovely harbingers of Christ join and sing,
    With your charming voices transcendent fling ;
    Our dear Savior died that all might live,
    Sun and twilight, our hearts to him we give.

12  As twilight glides mid ethereal blue,
    She calls, and waves her golden tresses, too,
    I seek repose in the flowering vale,
    O'er great towering mountains, and the dale.

13    While charming sirens sing the dirge of day,
      Another will appear in bright array
      And guide all through the busy scenes of life.
      All through the world's highway of wealth and
         strife.

14    Can sirens sing to please all folks on earth,
      In sun and twilight all work may prove dearth.
      The most joyful song known for all to sing,
      Sun and fair twilight lovely treasures bring.

Chant 40.

## From the Rhyming Soldier's Chant,

### Eradiates Bright Cheering Rays of Light.

## ON EVENING'S DUSK,—DUSTY BREZEE,

And all Critics that attack him and his book entitled
"D. H. MORRISON'S PASTIME."

1    Did anybody ever see,
      Dictator as I prove to be,
        Dictator of the pen now hear,
        Morrison's pen I never fear.

2    Along the † lines I sound my call,
      The Rhyming Soldier now must fall !
        I'll bury him in evening's * dusk,
        For picking † corn and leaving * husk.

3    Dick blows his bugle louder still,
      Denounce the Rhyming Soldier's quill,
        No metre in his book you know,
        For him no mercy will I show.

4    Dick blows his bugle loud again,
      Now Morrison's Rhyme shall be slain,
        For in his book there is no feet,
        And I deride his soldier's * feet.

5   The lost Alpena on the lake,
    And pains with † Statesman he did take.
      Morrison wrote Milwaukee too,
      Milwaukee o'er the water blue.

6   Dick blows his bugle to his fill,
    The Rhyming Soldier shall be still,
      And all this world of me shall hear,
      His chants so bright I never fear.

### REPLY.

1   The Rhyming Soldier's turn has come,
    His truthful pen is ready from,
      From light of morn to evening's dusk,
      To pick the corn and leave the husk.

2   In self defence I now array,
    To match Dictator on his way.
      Such great ignorance never blow,
      Words of sense prove a better show.

3   All loving critics now hear me,
    Metreless chant is known to be,
      Please turn to Webster and you'll see
      The fool yourself has proved to be.

4   Musical words with no metre,
    *Darling critics note this feature,*
      No metre Webster asks of me,
      I hear to Webster not to thee.

5   Make no light of veterans brave,
    Our mother country they did save,
      Their good work nor manhood too
      Oh such disgrace will never do.

6   As Dick derides the soldier's feet,
    All folks with contempt Dick will treat.
      For Dick this chant loudly thunders,
      Just exposing his great blunders.

7    Please turn to Morrison's Pastime*
     Sweet critics there are found in rhyme,
        My light for Christians I defend,
        Against all thrash inferiors send.

8    Wise critics great that grant no bliss,
     Methinks I hear something like this:
        *You'll die the same ye wicked clan,*
        *As wicked Haman that bad man.*

MORAL.

     Sixteenth of Luke none heed your call,
     Verse twenty-four is where you fall.

---

∴ Along the lines I sound my call, refering to the army he has found
    a soldier.
* Dictator of the pen, Detroit Evening Journal and all other critics.
† Picking Corn Chant.
* Husk metre.
* Soldier's feet.  Abusing the author as soldier.
† Statesman, Garfield.
* Morrison Pastime.  His book

Chant 41.

## My Recreation.

1  For recreation I roamed one pleasant day,
   In Dayton I gleaned the most effulgent ray,
   In mystic favor two bright, loving angels stand,
   As they were sculptured by an ingenious hand.

2  We know sculptors inscribe the honor of our land,
   Prepared in life for dear life is sure to strand.
   Those angels convinced me I must surely go
   Where beautiful monuments point and friends lie
        low.

3  We feel to write as our Savior in love hath said,
   Love one another, and we think of the dead.
   Oh, the last line inscribed on the lofty church spire,
   That angels may look on it, sing and play the lyre.

4  Dear friends our mission perchance is Heaven's
        decree,
   That we should traverse delightful lands and the sea,
   And consign the lustre to all that merit bright,
   May such be our mission, it's our greatest delight.

Chant 42.

## Soldier's Home.

1 Dear and trustworthy servant for years of mine,
I pity such a sad countenance as thine,
As you've been roaming forlorn and sedate,
Now cheer up and tell me your troubles of late.


2 Kind benefactor must I be seen by you,
When so melancholy it never will do ;
I frankly admit I'm troubled in mind,
Friends and contentment I never can find.


3 Why, brave defender, this home is your boon of
bliss,
And in time of need, there's no place like this;
Now, brave defender, this home I furnish you,
Why not seek rest within and contentment, too.


4 O, merciful thou art to all soldiers like me ;
Now, my mind from trouble and sorrow I'll free.
O, why should I grieve for friends far away,
O, such grief, my trouble will never allay.


5 Now, brave defender, no one shall amand thee,
With a zealous eye your condition I see.
In sympathy consider me your best friend.
Cast all the past aside and there it will end.


6 Now my cup of great bliss is overflowing,
As I receive all bliss you are bestowing.
Fierce and tempestuous storms may rage without.
But I rest in your harbor, safe, with no doubt.

## View of Charming Siron and her Lovely Isle.

1   Mild and lovely star, Siron's Isle so bright,
    Heaven's rays on thy graceful form doth light,
    Heaven's breeze thy sweet perfume wafts with
       joy,
    O'er bright blue waters, as angels deploy.

2   Thy pleasing look enjoyment doth tender,
    On Dame Nature's mission in great splendor,
    Thy sweet perfume of Nature's joyful breeze.
    Fragrant with Nature's jewels all doth please.

3   I anchor my life boat and step ashore,
    Viewing your romantic scenery all o'er.
    On terra firma's great Acme I ask,
    Can I describe your beauty, doubtful task.

4   From the world's greatest height, I wish to speak,
    I see all from this highest mountain peak,
    With spy glass I view battle fields of yore,
    Where war decided all as blood did pour.

5   The question that chained poor mortal slave,
    But all were freed by conquerors brave,
    Also the question of oppression bold,
    And questions too numerous to be told.

6   Dear Siron of bright Isle, much have I seen.
    High mountains and low valleys, white and green,
    As I journey on, of more may I dream,
    Of your beauty and nature's crystal stream.

7   Comparing earth and ethereal blue,
    I think of nymphs, fairies and sirens, too,
    Yes, how they cheer this world both night and
      day,
    We refer to them all along our way.

Chant 44.

## Representation of Picture "From Shore to Shore."

1 As I chance to glean from bright crystal stream,
  I must define with all that prove extreme,
  And with such the most exact precision,
  Now in case I err, demand revision.

2 My mind inspired for yonder taper,
  My fervent zeal cheered on with favor,
  To seize and hold the most effulgent theme,
  Methinks I hear Genius advance extreme.

3 With time we row gently o'er life's great wave,
  May our Savior pilot, for he'll save;
  He'll save us in His mansion of rest,
  Where all Christians are forever blest.

4 Some in fancy writes the clown's desire,
  But with my pen may I prove much higher;
  Oh, how few advance and with success obtain
  The brightest taper and light the height of fame.

5 Associates seem like angels with me,
  While we are sailing o'er life's raging sea.
  In friendship joined, each so fondly clasped,
  We prize the bright future more than the past.

6 All are assigned their lot as proves to be
  Some adventurous risk all on the sea,
  Their frail craft so light is driven beyond
  The harbor fame they sought but never found.

7 Jesus, our captain, we'll keep in sight,
  And as we advance, oh such cheering light,
  Jesus is calling, come on, come on to me.
  Angels in heaven wait to welcome thee.

Chant 45.

# Battle of Gettysburg.

1 In the far away past I see bright isles and raging seas,
  Thermopalæ shines as a star on the brow of Greece,
  And famous Waterloo shines in military hue,
  And other scenes of military grandeur rise too.

2 The greatest heroes on the orbits of time display
  The brightest laurels known on the warrior's highway.
  Those warriors on the great pinnacle of fame now
        stand
  Honored with Meade and other heroes of our land.

3 Gettysburg heroes enrolled on the page of fame,
  In all radiance warriors honored her name.
  Rise not ye up ye honored dead that lie in the grave,
  Charge not with cavalry; our flag in triumph doth
        wave.

4 While honor guards with solemn tread, comrades
        know,
  Of your silent bivouacs on land and where waters flow.
  In your country's bright devotion warriors live all
  Civilization pays homage and brave deeds recall.

5 Bivouacs of heroes where lie many honored dead,
  We now paint, as it were, all drops of blood you've
        shed,
  As you have won the laurel of Gettysburg so bright.
  Gettysburg, our Waterloo, eradiates such light.

6 Great military effulgence to the world her fight,
  Disputed soil drank the blood of thousands day and
        night
  Fighting with all their might and main o'er that
        sacred spot,
  Her cemetery, the victory won, will never be forgot.

7 At last the conquered rebel, Lee, gave up the field,
  Many sad hearts that day before our guns had to yield.
  Of Gettysburg, great heroes this world in praise will
        speak,
  As her bright glory across the horizon doth streak.

Chant 46.

## The Author's Love Letter to Crank's Evening News.

1 Crank's Evening News has loudly rang,
And echoed forth its poisonous fang,
Paid twenty thousand for its slang, *
To friends that played and sweetly sang.

2 Crank's with gloves and fingers yellow,
They've lied about one fellow,
A fellow known of good repute,
Such foolish lies I now refute.

3 It's near the river, pure and bright,
Those foolish cranks take their delight.
They spin their webs both night and day,
To catch the pure that come their way.

Detroit, Mich.

---

* Libel.

Chant 47.

## Little David and Goliath.

### SAMUEL, CHAPTER 17.

1 All Philistines gathered for battle,
As they left their herds of sheep and cattle,
And King Saul pitched in battle array,
In the Valley of Elah one great day.

2 On mountains both armies stood side by side,
As the great Philistine Giant defied
To fight him then, and that should decide,
Then the great victor in triumph should ride.

3 With a helmet of brass upon his head,
With great defiance to David he said :
Am I a dog for a stripling to fight ?
All Israel but David heard with fright.

4   Little David arose and quickly said :
    A promise with Israel I have made,
    My promise with Israel I'll keep,
    For this purpose I've left my father's sheep.

5   Now the champion's shield is borne before,
    He challenging all Israel of yore.
    Says David the great Goliath I'll slay,
    Birds and beasts on his flesh will surely prey.

6   Whoever kills Goliath sure as my life,
    May have my beautiful daughter for wife,
    And great freedom I'll bestow upon you,
    On your father's house, all Israel too.

7   I David a lion and bear did slay,
    And Goliath I'll kill this very day,
    The wonderful Giant so very strong,
    His flesh I'll give to the birds for their song.

8   As the great Goliath came and drew near,
    His shout of defiance David did hear,
    Little David with his sling threw a stone,
    He killed Goliath his just atone.

9   Goliath's head he severed with sword,
    Then Israel's king could well afford
    All he promised David and his kin,
    The army of Philistines fled from him.

10   Now to Jerusalem David did go,
    And the head of Goliath he did show.
    King Saul said to the captain who is this,
    Abner whose stripling confering such bliss ?

11   Says Saul to David, who art thou, young man ?
    The son of Jesse, my battle no sham.
    My promise with Israel I did keep,
    Here is Goliath's head, in peace now sleep.

12 Fair damsels said by Saul thousands were slain,
David slew tens of thousands to obtain
King Saul's reward for the champion's head,
But the jealous king wished David dead.

13 As Johnathan shot his arrows we know,
And beyond David his arrows did go.
'Twas to save his life from ungrateful Saul,
David conquered his enemies all.

Chant 48.

## My Mission.

1 My mission is labor far and near,
For the good of all I'd have you hear.
Placing Christian light along the way,
So none from Christ will ever stray.

2 As I journey on earth here below,
See the demon's cup of poisonous flow,
And numerous vices all can name,
I'd gladly stop all sin and shame.

3 Bethlehem's star is shining bright,
All along the Christian's path of light.
I warn all sinners of their fall,
Those proving deaf to Christ's dear call.

4 I'll labor in this cause that's right,
Point sinners to God's mansion bright,
To Heaven's host a precious sight,
Where all is day, there is no night.

5 All shun the poisonous cup of sin,
In God's fold all now enter in,
Enjoy God's boon now from above,
So deeds will shine with God's pure love.

6    I'll labor on dear Christian friends,
     For this world's good so happiness blends,
     With minds of mortals here below,
     That journey here both to and fro.


7    Friends our mission please bear in mind,
     It s to convert all souls we can find,
     All sinners on the road so dark,
     Give heed to conscience's glowing spark


Chant 49.

## Discretion.

Shall I write void of measure for the sake of wisdom,
Or write void of wisdom for the sake of measure ?
All friends on earth please answer at your pleasure.


Chant 50.

## Who Is My Friend ?

1    Will any mortal prove my friend ?
     Will you kind reader now please lend
     A listening ear so thoughts may blend,
     With friendship void of selfish end.


2    Passing along this world's highway,
     It's many times I've heard folks say
     I hate the poor, they shall not stay,
     In my good home no night nor day.

3  God's angels watches over all,
   Please read our blessed Savior's call,
   Sixteenth of Luke, this part is best,
   Hard hearted mortals just to test.


4  My friend my word does not deride,
   Nor my good character beside,
   My friend to mercy does incline,
   Read James the second and verse nine.


5  My loving friend will e'er say no,
   When a kind heart much might bestow
   To cheer me here on earth below,
   As I journey on both to and fro.


6  My friend's the one that has a heart,
   My friend a blessing will impart,
   My friend'll cool my fevered brain,
   My frame of life will help sustain.


Chant 51.

## The Printer.

1 Of all I've wrote and all I've found,
  There's one the greatest in renown;
  It's known the printer far and near,
  When type is still naught do we hear


2 God bless all printers on their way,
  Their work is great—oftimes no pay—
  To all this world a cheering light,
  And for the same sometimes they fight.

# CONTENTS.

www.ingramcontent.com/pod-product-compliance
Lightning Source LLC
Chambersburg PA
CBHW020236090426
42735CB00010B/1713